make it in
Minutes

Last-Minute Gifts

make it in
Minutes

Last-Minute Gifts

TAYLOR HAGERTY

LARK BOOKS

A Division of Sterling Publishing Co., Inc.
New York / London

Book Editor
Catherine Risling

Copy Editor
Ashlea Scaglione

Photographers
Mark Tanner
Zachary Williams

Stylist
Rebecca Ittner

Book Designer
Kehoe+Kehoe Design
Associates

A Red Lips 4 Courage Communications, Inc., book
www.redlips4courage.com
Eileen Cannon Paulin
President
Catherine Risling
Director of Editorial

Library of Congress Cataloging-in-Publication Data

Hagerty, Taylor.
    Make it in minutes. Last-minute gifts / Taylor Hagerty. — 1st ed.
        p. cm.
    Includes index.
    ISBN-13: 978-1-60059-316-1 (hc-plc with concealed spiral : alk. paper)
    ISBN-10: 1-60059-316-X (hc-plc with concealed spiral : alk. paper)
    1. Handicraft. 2. Gifts. I. Title. II. Title: Last-minute gifts.
    TT157.H2727 2008
    745.5—dc22

                                    2007046453

10 9 8 7 6 5 4 3 2 1

First Edition

Published by Lark Books, A Division of
Sterling Publishing Co., Inc.
387 Park Avenue South, New York, NY 10016

Text © 2008, Taylor Hagerty
Photography © 2008, Red Lips 4 Courage Communications, Inc.
Illustrations © 2008, Red Lips 4 Courage Communications, Inc.

Distributed in Canada by Sterling Publishing,
c/o Canadian Manda Group, 165 Dufferin St.
Toronto, Ontario, Canada M6K 3H6

Distributed in the United Kingdom by GMC Distribution Services,
Castle Place, 166 High St., Lewes, East Sussex, England BN7 1XU

Distributed in Australia by Capricorn Link (Australia) Pty Ltd.,
P.O. Box 704, Windsor, NSW 2756 Australia

If you have questions or comments about this book, please contact:
Lark Books
67 Broadway
Asheville, NC 28801
(828) 253-0467

Manufactured in China

ISBN-13: 978-1-60059-316-1

For information about custom editions, special sales, premium and corporate pur-
chases, please contact Sterling Special Sales Department at (800) 805-5489 or
specialsales@sterlingpub.com.

"I have found that among its other benefits,
giving liberates the soul of the giver."
—Maya Angelou

Contents

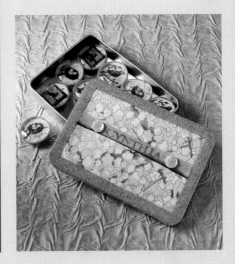

YOU ARE INVITED
TO CELEBRATE

LOVE

10 P.M.

LEVEL: UPPER, SECTION 203
ROW II, SEATS 7-8

Introduction

With this book as your resource, there's no reason to arrive at a party empty-handed, to forget to pick up a birthday gift, or to simply not have the right gesture to convey a heartfelt thank you. With a few crafting supplies, some fabulous ribbon, decorative paper, glitter, and more, you can create any of the fun and creative projects in this book.

You can fashion a gift from linen or paper, or create one-of-a-kind home accents or jewelry accessories designed with the recipient in mind. And when your gift is rather simple, like a gift card or favorite packets of tea, we have a few ideas for eye-catching gift wrap anyone would adore.

Of course, few things speak from the heart like a lovely handmade gift with a friend's favorite colors and style in mind. The best part is that each gift can be made in less than an hour, making these ideas perfect for last-minute gift giving.

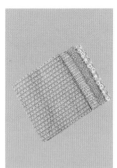

CHAPTER 1

If you're like me, you just can't resist luscious ribbons, pretty decorative papers, and papier-mâché shapes that seem to beg to be part of a project. In addition to the new, you may also love the old—vintage books, trims, stamps, or other ephemera. All of these elements—in addition to a few basic tools and supplies—are all you need to create the dozens of projects featured throughout this book.

In this chapter you'll find a primer on the adhesives, tools, and embellishments you will need, in addition to a few basic techniques to master the craft of creating these last-minute projects. Familiarize yourself with these essentials and prepare to create dazzling gifts that look as though they took much longer than an hour to make.

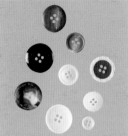

Embellishments

Beads
Found in all parts of the world in an enormous variety of materials, sizes, and shapes, beads add a perfect finishing touch. From glittering crystal to natural bone, beads can be functional or simply decorative.

Buttons
Available in many different sizes, colors, and finishes, buttons add a wonderful dimensional element to any project. Sew or glue them onto projects for the perfect finishing touch.

Costume jewelry, rhinestones, and sequins
Add a sparkly accent to projects by using faceted rhinestones or glittering sequins, or repurpose costume jewelry for a starring role in a thoughtful gift. Adhering rhinestones and sequins with craft glue or glue dots is easy and fun.

Decorative paper
Decorative paper isn't limited to just scrapbook paper. There are all kinds of cardstock, chipboard, fabric-backed paper, mulberry, parchment, tissue, and wallpaper available to enhance gifts with color, texture, and beauty. Try using ephemera such as stamps, tea-stained ledger paper, or old postcards for a sense of romantic.

Fabric
Cloth adds a tactile depth and warmth to a project. It is a wonderful way to personalize a gift. Whether you choose a sturdy gingham for a cook's gift, a playful cotton print for a child, leather for a masculine presentation, or silk for the utmost femininity, the use of fabric in a project is limited only by your imagination.

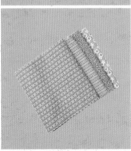

Glitter
A dusting of glitter adds an elegant touch and never fails to be the center of attention. Glitter is available in various forms, from superfine to chunky, mica powders and flakes, and even crushed real glass. *Note:* Be careful when using glass glitter because it is literally shards of glass and will cut you if you're not careful. Use double-sided tape, craft glue, or adhesive paper to adhere glitter and add some sparkle to a project.

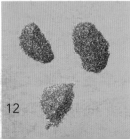

Jewelry findings

The basic elements of jewelry making include chains, clasps, drop pins, earring wires, jump rings, spacers, and split rings. These items, coupled with beads, shells, stones, and other baubles, allow you to create a wide variety of bejeweled gifts.

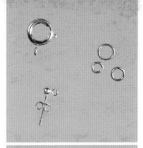

Natural elements

Use natural items in projects to create organic gifts. Items like feathers, pressed flowers, or seashells add a touch of the outdoors and some can literally be a breath of fresh air. Herbs and spices such as cinnamon, clove, eucalyptus, lavender, and rosemary, whether in their natural state or as essential oils, add a heady aroma to sachets, bath salts, and other aromatherapy gifts.

Office supplies

Project supplies are often found in unusual places such as an office supply store. Binder rings, clipboards, hole reinforcements, labels, poster board, shipping tags, and stationery with envelopes are the makings of truly memorable gifts.

Paint

Add color to a gift project with paint. Acrylic paint is excellent not only for painting but for stamping designs with rubber stamps. Watercolor paint adds a soft, colorful touch to paper elements. Even spray paint is good for fast coverage on larger objects.

Stickers and rub-ons

These two types of adhesive decals are found in an enormous variety of colors, shapes, and sizes. Stickers are designs printed on paper with an adhesive backing. Rub-ons are printed on the adhesive and applied to the project with a craft stick. Both are quick and easy to use for embellishing a project, adding words or titles, or spelling out the recipient's name on a card or tag.

Trims

Available in a mind-boggling variety of widths, colors, and materials, there is surely a trim for every type of gift imaginable. Embroidery floss, pom-pom trim, raffia, ribbon, rickrack, twine, and yarn all add different textural accents to gifts.

Tools

Bone folder

Craft scissors

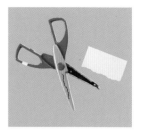

Decorative-edge scissors

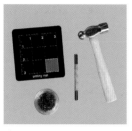

Eyelet setting tools

Heat tool

Hole punch

Paper punch

Paper trimmer

Pinking shears

Pliers

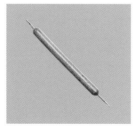

Scoring tool

Wire cutters

Adhesives

Acid-free adhesive dispenser
Acid-free adhesives are applicators containing a dry form of glue dispensed in a small dot or linear form. It can turn corners and bond papers with little or no puckering.

Adhesive dots
Adhesive dots have adhesive on both sides and are available in sizes ranging from ⅛" to ½". Regular glue dots are simply thin circles of strong adhesive and are a reliable way of reinforcing heavy elements on a project. Foam dots, however, are excellent for adding dimension to projects—stack two or more under embellishments for extra impact. There are also glue dots made especially for use with vellum so they don't show through the paper.

Decoupage glue
This multipurpose medium is a glue, sealant, and finish all in one. Use it to adhere paper elements to surfaces. While wet, clean up is easy with soap and water, and once dry, decoupage glue is water-resistant.

Double-sided tape
This clear tape has adhesive on both sides and works best for paper-to-paper applications. It comes in a variety of widths, and there are different strengths available, from the traditional double-sided type to tacky tape. Tacky tape is a stronger adhesive and works well with glitter and micro beads.

Hot glue gun and glue sticks
This adhesive works quickly and is quite strong on most surfaces. It is available in two forms: high-temp or hot glue and low-temp glue. Glue guns and the melted glue reach temperatures that can cause serious burns so use caution with this adhesive.

Spray adhesive
Applied in a similar manner as spray paint, spray adhesive offers a repositionable or permanent bond for many materials. The glue is a strong, water-resistant adhesive that dries permanently in approximately 30 minutes. Be sure to protect your work surface from overspray before applying this adhesive.

General Techniques

Creating sharp creases

To make a sharp crease using heavyweight paper or cardstock, use a scoring or embossing tool and a bone folder. Mark the top and bottom edges of the paper or cardstock where you want it to fold. Lay a metal-edged ruler on the marks and then firmly draw the scoring or embossing tool along the ruler's edge. Fold the paper along the crease line and, holding the bone folder perpendicular to the paper, draw it firmly across the length of the fold.

Heat embossing

Stamp an image on paper with embossing ink and then cover it with embossing powder (Fig. 1); make sure to tap off excess. Using a heat tool, melt the powder by holding it over the image 5–10 seconds (Fig. 2); allow to cool.

Inking edges

Create an aged effect by dragging the edges of a piece of paper or photograph across an inkpad and let dry. For a softer look, apply ink by patting a cosmetic sponge on the inkpad and then dabbing it lightly onto the edges or surface of the paper. This may require several applications for a more intense color.

Fig. 1

Fig. 2

time-saving tip

Keep It Contained

To speed up clean up, sprinkle embossing powder on project that's been placed inside a box. This will make pouring the powder back into the jar a lot easier—and quicker.

Jewelry Techniques

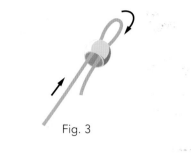

Fig. 3

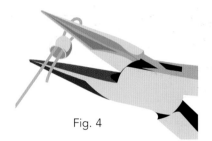

Fig. 4

Fig. 5

Crimping
Thread beading wire through the crimp bead, make a small loop, and then thread the wire back through the bead (Fig. 3). Flatten the crimp with the pliers until the bead holds the wire in place (Fig. 4). Test the wire to make sure it does not slip out of the bead.

Using jump rings
Grasp a jump ring on either side of the ring's opening using two pairs of pliers (Fig. 5). Pull one side of the ring toward you while twisting the other away from you until it's open wide enough (Fig. 6). To close the ring, twist the ring ends towards each other until they meet.

Fig. 6

Chain stitch

Fig. 1

Fig. 2

Fig. 3

French knot

Fig. 4

Fig. 5

Fig. 6

Stitches

The stitches used in the projects in this book are simple to do but require some practice if you've never used them before. It's a good idea to try the stitches on fabric scraps until you are comfortable and able to achieve consistent results.

■ *Chain stitch:* Working along a single stitch line, bring thread through to front of fabric (Fig. 1). Holding thread down with your non-sewing thumb, form a loop the desired size and then insert needle back through original hole (Fig. 2). Bring needle out opposite end of loop and, keeping thread under needle's point, pull loop of thread to form first chain (Fig. 3). Continue working stitches in same manner until you reach the desired length.

■ *French knot:* Bring thread through to front of fabric. Hold thread taut and wrap it twice around needle in clockwise direction (Fig. 4). Holding thread taut (Fig. 5), insert needle into fabric, close to point where it emerged. Pull needle and thread to back of fabric, leaving a loose knot at front (Fig. 6).

Lazy daisy: This stitch is similar to the chain stitch instructions but instead of working in a straight line, you are forming a simple flower. Bring thread through to front of fabric in spot where you want first petal. Holding thread down with your non-sewing thumb, form a loop the desired size and then insert needle back through original hole (Fig. 7). Bring needle back up through fabric on opposite end of loop, on inside of loop. Cross over loop and insert needle, making a very small stitch to hold loop in place (Fig. 8). Continue to work petals in a circle, forming a daisy. Tie off thread underneath fabric to complete pattern.

Whipstitch: Insert needle between two layers of fabric and bring through bottom fabric layer, sandwiching knotted end of thread (Fig. 9). Wrap thread around edge of layered fabric and insert needle in the top and a bit to the right of the bottom stitch (Fig. 10). Bring needle out directly below, making sure to keep thread under needle tip (Fig. 11). Pull thread through fabric and continue working in the same manner, making sure to space stitches evenly and at same height.

Lazy daisy

Fig. 7

Fig. 8

Whipstitch

Fig. 9

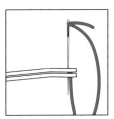

Fig. 10

Fig. 11

CHAPTER 2

It's not necessary to spend hours in order to craft an artistic masterpiece. You can create a gift in just a few minutes for an impression that will last much longer—your thoughtful consideration will shine through in the details. Embellish a hostess's table with monogrammed napkins; soothe a frazzled friend's nerves with wonderfully scented bath oil or salts; or welcome new neighbors to the community with lavender water to freshen their travel-weary bed linens. Whip up fragrant sachets using different herbs to scent a lingerie drawer. The aroma of flowers and herbs pampers the senses and soothes the psyche. Personalize your project with a monogram or hand-crafted tag that shows you chose the gift especially for the lucky recipient.

Monogrammed Napkins

Materials

- Acid-free adhesive dispenser
- Button: 1" black
- Craft scissors
- Embroidery thread: copper (12")
- Fabric ink: black
- Fabric marker: black
- Fabric paint: copper
- Fabric paper: black and copper patterned
- Foam brush
- Masking tape
- Napkins: cloth (4)
- Rubber stamp: monogram
- Ruler

Instructions

1. Using masking tape, mask off 1" around outer edges of napkins. With foam brush, apply copper fabric paint; let dry. Remove masking tape.

2. Draw dashed line with black fabric marker on edge of copper strip.

3. Stamp monogram rubber stamp with black fabric ink and stamp one corner of each napkin.

4. Cut fabric paper into 12"x 3" strip; fold ¾" of long edges toward backside of strip, creating decorative band. Wrap around folded napkins and adhere ends together with adhesive dispenser.

5. Tie copper embroidery thread through holes in button; knot on top and then trim excess. Adhere button to center of decorative strip using adhesive dispenser.

Silk Sachets

Materials

- Costume jewelry
- Fabric: silk
- Fresh eucalyptus leaves
- Lime peel
- Measuring spoons
- Ribbon: $\frac{1}{2}$" satin
- Ruler
- Sand
- Scissors: fabric, pinking shears

Instructions

1. Cut 10" circle out of fabric with pinking shears. *Note:* It's best to use a fabric that is not too heavy so that it can breath and allow the aroma to emanate.

2. Add 2 tablespoons of eucalyptus leaves and lime peel and 2 teaspoons of sand to center of circle. *Note:* The sand will act as an abrasive to release the scent of the potpourri.

3. Bring up sides of fabric around potpourri and cinch fabric with your fingers, right above the ball you've made.

4. Tie ribbon around fabric and into small knot, cinching it tightly to secure potpourri inside; trim ends with fabric scissors.

5. Pin on elegant brooch, pin, or large earring to finish.

time-saving tip

Fill Up Your Senses

The Silk Sachets can be slipped in a lingerie drawer or left on top of a pillow for a calming aroma at the end of a long day.

Lavender Pillow

Materials

- Dried lavender
- Fabric: coordinating prints 8" squares (2); tulle 8" square
- Fabric scissors
- Fiber fill
- Ribbon: ⅛" silk, coordinating colors (3)
- Ribbon needle
- Ruler
- Sewing machine
- Straight pins

Instructions

1. With narrow silk ribbon and ribbon needle, use lazy daisy stitch, stem stitch, and French knots to embroider simple flower with stem and leaves near lower right corner of 8" square of tulle, making sure to allow room for seam.

2. Sandwich tulle between two layers of printed fabrics with right sides facing. Using sewing machine, stitch layers together, leaving 4" opening.

3. Using fabric scissors, clip corners and turn pillow right side out with tulle on topside. Sprinkle dried lavender between layer of tulle and top fabric.

4. Fill pillow with fiber fill. Add dried lavender inside pillow.

5. Fold pillow opening in place; secure with straight pins. With coordinating silk ribbon and ribbon needle, stitch around all edges of pillow with whip stitch.

6. Tie simple bow around flower stem with remaining silk ribbon.

Herbal Bath Oil

Materials

- Bowl: medium-sized
- Cinnamon sticks (4)
- Computer, printer, and scanner
- Craft scissors
- Decorative paper
- Fresh rosemary (2 sprigs)
- Glass bottle
- Glue stick
- Ground cinnamon
- Image
- Inkpad: soft gold
- Measuring cup
- Measuring spoons
- Paper: white
- Ribbon: 1/4" coordinating satin
- Rosemary oil (10 drops)
- Ruler
- Spoon
- Unscented bath/body oil

Instructions

1. Crush cinnamon sticks and fresh rosemary together in medium-sized bowl and then mix in 1 tsp. of ground cinnamon. *Note:* The sticks of cinnamon and the rosemary don't have to be completely crushed, just enough to be fragrant.

2. Pour in 2 cups of lukewarm water. Add 10 drops of rosemary oil, then stir. Let mixture steep 30 minutes to infuse ingredients.

3. Pour infused water into bottle, filling only a quarter of bottle.

4. Tip bottle at 45-degree angle; pour bath/body oil in slowly on top of infused water to fill rest of bottle.

5. **To make label:** Cut 2"x 3" rectangle out of decorative paper. Using computer and scanner, print desired image on white paper. Cut around image to create 1"x 1½" rectangle. Ink edges with gold ink. Glue label to center of decorative paper; glue to bottle. Wrap ribbon around bottle and label, knotting it in place.

Lavender Water

Materials

- ⅛" hole punch
- Container: medium-sized
- Crystal bead
- Decorative paper
- Decorative-edge scissors
- Distilled water
- Essential lavender oil
- Long spoon
- Measuring cup
- Old bottle with cork top
- Ribbon: 1" lavender satin
- String
- Vodka: 2 oz.

Instructions

1. Mix 2 cups of distilled water and 2 oz. of vodka in medium-sized container.

2. Add 10 drops of lavender oil; stir mixture slowly with spoon. Fill bottle with mixture and replace top or cork, depending on type of bottle.

3. **To make tag:** Using decorative-edge scissors, cut desired shape out of decorative paper; punch hole at top, add string to center, and embellish with crystal bead.

4. Tie ribbon in bow around bottleneck. Tie on tag.

time-saving tip

A Sprinkle a Day

The scent of the Lavender Water may be quite strong at first, but time will lessen the intensity. The water can be sprinkled on pillows, furniture, carpet, or even fresh linens as they're being ironed.

Rosy Bath Salts

Materials

- Beeswax
- Cardstock
- Computer and printer
- Craft scissors
- Craft wire: 24–gauge
- Glass jar with cork stopper
- Glue stick
- Hot glue gun and glue sticks
- Inkpads: green, pink
- Measuring cup
- Melting pot
- Metal spoon
- Mineral salts
- Parchment paper
- Plastic bowl
- Ribbon: ½" coordinating (2)
- Rubber stamp: rose
- Ruler
- Shipping tags: small (2)
- Silk flower
- Soap colorant
- Soap scent
- Velvet leaves (9)
- Wooden spoon

Instructions

1. In a plastic bowl, stir 2 drops of soap scent into a cup of mineral salts using wooden spoon. Mix in 2–3 drops of soap colorant. *Note:* You may continue to mix in 1–2 drops of colorant at a time until desired color is achieved.

2. Fill glass jar with mineral salts; insert cork back into bottle.

3. Cover your work surface with parchment paper. Melt beeswax in melting pot.

time-saving tip

Scents with Benefits

Mix dried flowers or herbs into the bath salts for added benefits. Lavender is soothing, while mint is invigorating. An Internet search will provide a wealth of information on bath flowers and herbs.

A rose in full bloom makes the Rosy Bath Salts jar pretty from all angles.

time-saving tip

Pillow Top

Another fun idea for adorning the top of the Rosy Bath Salts jar is to wrap a square piece of fabric around the cork and secure it in place with coordinating ribbon. You could also add filler such as foam or cotton batting under the fabric for a dimensional look.

4. Place jar on parchment paper. Fill metal spoon with melted wax and drip over top of cork to secure in place. Continue dripping wax over cork until you are satisfied with the look of the jar; let wax cool.

5. Hot glue velvet leaves and silk flower on top of cork; let cool.

6. Stamp rose image on one of the shipping tags with pink and green ink; ink edges.

7. Using computer, print sentiment onto cardstock; cut out and ink edges. Adhere to remaining shipping tag with glue stick.

8. Measure and cut craft wire to wrap around jar three times, leaving 4" tails. Thread shipping tags onto ends of craft wire and twist wire to secure tags in place.

9. Cut both ribbons long enough to wrap around neck of jar and tie into a bow. Tie ribbons around jar and tie on shipping tags.

Small shipping tags are edged with an inkpad for an aged appearance.

time-saving tip

Get Closure

You may also use a screw-top jar to hold the bath salts. Just fill the jar and replace the lid. Using a screw top will eliminate the need for a wax seal.

Tea Towels

Materials

- Craft scissors
- Decorative braid
- Iron and ironing board
- Ribbon: ³⁄₈" coordinating
- Sewing needle
- Straight pins (12)
- Tea towels (3)
- Thread: coordinating

Instructions

1. Wash and iron tea towels.

2. Measure and cut ribbon to fit width of tea towels.

3. Using straight pins, secure ribbon in place at varying distances from edges of tea towels.

4. Stitch ribbon to towel using needle and thread; repeat with other towels.

5. Lay decorative braid over top of stitched ribbon; stitch in place.

time-saving tip

Skip the Stitches

To save time and stitches, eliminate the ribbon and just stitch the decorative braid directly onto the tea towels.

Lingerie Bag

Materials

- Fabric scissors
- Iron and ironing board
- Lace edging
- Linen: off-white
- Ribbon: $\frac{1}{8}$" silk
- Ruler
- Sewing machine (optional)
- Sewing needle
- Straight pins (12)
- Thread: off-white

Instructions

1. Cut linen into two 8" x 18" rectangles. With rectangles layered, find center point of one narrow end; mark with straight pin. Measure 4" from edge of same end; mark with another pin. Repeat on opposite side to form an inverted V, as indicated by red lines (see Diagram A). Cut corners away with fabric scissors.

2. With straight stitch on sewing machine or by hand stitching, sew layers together, leaving a $\frac{1}{2}$" seam allowance on all sides and a 3" opening for turning the fabric.

3. Turn fabric by pulling inside out through opening. Press flat with iron set to linen setting.

4. Fold rectangular section in half to form a square with V-shaped flap extending beyond. Hand stitch sides together with needle and thread.

5. Embellish bottom and top of bag and flap by stitching on 24" length of lace edging. Thread 24" length of silk ribbon through lace; tie small bow at base of flap.

Diagram A

CHAPTER 3

Paper gifts have traditionally been the province of the first wedding anniversary. In today's fast-paced electronic world, gifts crafted from paper are touchingly nostalgic. A gift of note cards or stationery will allow the recipient to convey affectionate greetings. A pre-decorated photo album is an ideal gift for new parents capturing precious moments of a new life. An embellished recipe book, complete with a recipe or two and space to add more, is perfect for a new bride. Revive a Victorian tradition and create personalized calling cards for new neighbors or co-workers. Luggage tags for a favorite world traveler will make suitcases easy to spot on the airport's baggage carousel. Pass along sweet sentiments with paper-wrapped candy bars. Release your inner paper crafter with any of these innovative projects and make a delightful paper gift for someone special.

Paper

Photo Album

Materials

- Acrylic stamps: outline of journaling boxes
- Adhesives: acid-free adhesive dispenser, glue stick
- Cardstock: off-white
- Chipboard mini-album: 3-ring binder style
- Cosmetic sponges
- Craft scissors
- Decorative papers: coordinating prints (4–5)
- Hole reinforcements
- Inkpads: black, brown
- Paper trimmer
- Pencil
- Photo corners
- Ribbon: ½" organdy
- Ruler
- Sandpaper: medium-grit

Instructions

1. Using blank chipboard album cover as a template, trace on decorative papers to fit outside and inside of covers; cut using paper trimmer. Cut additional strip to cover outside spine of album and to wrap around front and back covers. Cut coordinating papers to fit all inside pages.

2. Adhere paper to cover and pages with glue stick and then sand edges smooth. Apply brown ink to edges with cosmetic sponge, if desired.

3. Cut one 3" square for each page from various coordinating papers. Apply brown ink to edges, and then adhere to pages at an angle.

4. Using acrylic stamps and black ink, stamp journaling box on off-white cardstock; cut out and apply ink to edges. Adhere journaling boxes to half of the 3" squares and photo corners on facing pages with adhesive dispenser. Ink hole reinforcements with brown ink and apply to binder ring holes. Tie two lengths of ribbon on left edges of cover; knot and trim ends.

Stationery Portfolio

Materials

- Acid-free adhesive dispenser
- Blank stationery: off-white cards and envelopes (6–8)
- Cardstock: off-white, purple
- Cosmetic sponge
- Craft scissors
- Decorative paper
- Embossing ink: coordinating
- Embossing powder: coordinating
- Heat gun
- Inkpad: coordinating color
- Paper trimmer
- Pencil
- Ribbon: ½" silk
- Rubber stamp
- Ruler
- Scoring tool

Instructions

1. **To embellish stationery:** Cut ½" strip of decorative paper, ink edges with cosmetic sponge, and adhere around lower section of folded card. Stamp image with embossing ink onto 2" square piece of off-white cardstock, coat with embossing powder, and heat with heat gun until melted. Mat with decorative paper and then mount to front of card over paper strip with adhesive dispenser.

2. **To line envelopes:** Using open envelope as template, trace and cut out shape from decorative paper; trim ¼" off all edges. Insert into envelope, lining up with flap; adhere in place with adhesive dispenser.

3. **To create portfolio:** Cut purple cardstock to 12"x 8". Score and crease at 1", 4¾", 5¼", and 11". Fold creases at 1" and 11" towards inside; adhere with adhesive dispenser only at top and bottom, creating a narrow pocket. *Note:* The center scores will create a gusset.

4. **To embellish portfolio cover:** Cut ¾" strip of decorative paper, ink edges with cosmetic sponge, and adhere around cover. Adhere 24" length of ribbon with adhesive dispenser over paper strip, allowing ends to extend off cover. Repeat second part of step 1 to create embossed embellishment; adhere over ribbon.

5. Insert cards into left side of open portfolio and envelopes into right side. Close and tie ribbon into a simple bow to secure.

Candy Bars

Materials

- Adhesives: glitter adhesive, glue stick
- Candy bars
- Colored foil
- Craft scissors
- Decorative paper: coordinating prints (2)
- Glitter: super-fine, coordinating color
- Pencil

Instructions

1. Carefully remove paper wrapper and foil from candy bars.

2. Trace original wrappers on new colored foil and decorative paper; cut out.

3. Wrap candy bar with new colored foil, making sure entire bar is covered.

4. Wrap decorative paper around candy bar snugly, overlapping ends and securing closed with glue stick. *Note:* Be sure you don't glue the decorative paper to the foil.

5. Using glitter adhesive, add glitter in shapes like circles or straight lines (refer to project photo). Cut out other shapes from coordinating decorative paper and adhere on new wrapper using glue stick.

time-saving tip

Reason to Party

An excellent project for an upcoming holiday party or a birthday party for a friend, the Candy Bars make ideal party favors or they may be placed on a table as decoration.

Recipe Book

Materials

- ¼" hole punch
- Adhesives: double-sided tape, spray adhesive
- Binder ring
- Cardstock: cream, double-sided (2)
- Chipboard: 6" square (2)
- Computer and printer
- Cosmetic sponge
- Craft scissors
- Decorative paper
- Die-cut words
- Inkpad: brown
- Measuring spoons
- Rhinestone
- Ribbon: assorted colors (4–5)
- Rub-on stickers
- Ruler

Instructions

1. Cut one 12" x 12" sheet of double-sided cardstock into four squares. Adhere with spray adhesive to front and back of two 6" square pieces of chipboard.

2. Die-cut letters out of cream cardstock and adhere to book front. Embellish with rub-on stickers and add rhinestone as accent mark on "i" in "appetit." Tie 18" length of ribbon around book front.

3. Cut remaining double-sided cardstock into 6" squares.

4. Using computer, print out recipes to fit within a $4\frac{1}{2}$" square on decorative paper. Trim and adhere to cardstock with double-sided tape. Ink edges with cosmetic sponge as desired.

5. Align pages and cover and punch hole in upper left hand corner. Add binder ring and tie on 6" pieces of coordinating ribbon. Clip measuring spoons to ring.

time-saving tip

Add Some Weight

You can add as many pages to the Recipe Book as you like. The only limit is the size of the binder ring.

Coasters

Materials

- Corkboard
- Craft scissors
- Decorative paper: coordinating prints (3)
- Foil tape
- Glass circles: coaster size (3)
- Glue stick
- Pencil
- Poster board
- Pressed flowers

Instructions

1. Using glass circle, trace shape onto piece of poster board, decorative paper, and corkboard; cut out and then set corkboard aside. Adhere poster board and decorative paper circles together with glue stick.

2. Glue pressed flower on top of decorative paper in pleasing display. Glue corkboard onto poster board side of circle.

3. Lay piece of glass on top of decorative paper and press foil tape securely around edges to finish.

4. Repeat steps 1–3 to complete set of coasters.

time-saving tip

Widen Your Search

If you find that glass circles are not readily available in your area, consider having them cut at your local glass shop. Also, there are several online sources that carry glass in various sizes.

Wallpaper Note Cards

Materials

- Blank note cards and envelopes (4–6)
- Craft scissors
- Glue stick
- Pencil
- Wallpaper: coordinating patterns (2)

Instructions

1. Measure inside of envelope by placing square of wallpaper over envelope and tracing around it; cut out shape. *Note:* Make sure to cut around the part where there's glue.

2. Open up note card and lay it flat on a piece of wallpaper; trace note card and then cut out. Repeat to create desired number of note cards.

3. Glue patterns in appropriate positions (inside envelope or around outside of note card); let dry completely.

4. Place note card of one pattern with the envelope of another pattern.

time-saving tip

All Tied Up

Step up the creativity by tying your bundle of Wallpaper Note Cards with a wide, elegant silk ribbon.

Calling Cards

Materials

- ⅛" hole punch
- Bone folder
- Cardstock: coordinating (4)
- Computer and printer
- Decorative-edge scissors: scalloped
- Glue stick
- Paper trimmer
- Pencil

Instructions

Note: Following instructions yield 24 cards.

1. Using bone folder, divide cardstock in half lengthwise and into four widthwise. Trace fold marks with pencil.

2. Using paper trimmer, cut along pencil lines, making eight cards from each sheet. Trim edges with decorative-edge scissors.

3. Using computer, print name and e-mail address or phone number on coordinating cardstock; cut out and adhere to calling cards.

4. Make dot inside each scallop with a pencil; make hole at each dot using hole punch.

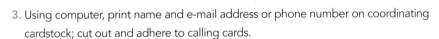

time-saving tip

Mix it Up

You may want to vary the "lace" patterns on the edges of each card by using different-sized scalloped scissors—some make a "lacier" pattern than others.

Luggage Tags

Materials

- ½" hole punch
- Adhesive laminating paper
- Adhesives: glue stick, hook-and-loop dot, strong-hold glue
- Computer and printer
- Craft scissors
- Heavyweight decorative paper: coordinating patterned (2); solid color
- Paper punch: corner rounder
- Pencil
- Ribbon: ½" coordinating grosgrain
- Ruler

Instructions

1. Using a ruler and pencil, trace and cut out two 2" x 8" rectangles from patterned paper. Fold in half lengthwise, ending up with two 2" x 4" pieces; round off edges with paper punch.

2. Adhere adhesive laminating paper to both sides of tags, adding an extra ¼" to edges.

3. Using computer, print name, address, and phone number on one side of decorative paper; print monogram on opposite side so that when card is folded, it appears on front. Laminate card then fold in half and trim to create 2" x 1" card. Add hook-and-loop dot to keep card closed; add card to front of luggage tag with strong-hold adhesive.

4. Punch hole on short side of luggage tag; thread 20" length of ribbon through hole and knot ends.

time-saving tip

The Stronger the Better

To create even sturdier tags, try adding layers of the adhesive laminate until it reaches the thickness you prefer.

CHAPTER 4

Transform the ordinary into the extraordinary with a few basic crafting supplies. A store-bought pillar candle can become a sweet tribute to family members with a layering of decorative paper, ribbon, and a favorite photograph sized to fit. Customize a glass paperweight base with a paper monogram. Flat-backed clear marbles embellished with favorite images become magnets to hold the daily to-do and shopping lists in style. Matchboxes decorated with patterned papers and trims can do double duty by holding tiny gifts or sitting on a desktop holding small knickknacks. An embellished birdhouse is a clever housewarming gift, and a clipboard becomes command central with envelope pockets for keeping track of the household's daily life. In this chapter there's a home decor gift for just about any occasion.

Paperweight

Materials

- Adhesives: craft glue, glue stick
- Cording
- Decorative paper: coordinating pattern, solid color
- Felt: coordinating color
- Inkpad: black
- Old stamps (2)
- Paper letter
- Paperweight kit
- Pencil
- Ribbon: 1/2" silk taupe
- Ruler
- Scissors: craft, pinking shears
- Textured paper: white

Instructions

1. Trace paperweight on patterned paper; cut out.

2. Cut 4" x 1" piece of solid color decorative paper. Cut 4" length of ribbon. Layer and adhere ribbon and paper strip to decorative paper with glue stick; trim edges.

3. Cut 1½" square piece of textured paper. Adhere letter on top with glue stick and then glue on top of ribbon.

4. Overlap old stamps and adhere at bottom of textured paper with glue stick.

5. Following paperweight kit instructions, assemble paperweight, decorative paper, mounting board, and bottom pad.

6. Trace paperweight on felt; cut out slightly larger using pinking shears. Adhere to bottom of paperweight using craft glue. Adhere cording around base of paperweight with craft glue.

Magnet Set

Materials

- Acrylic paint: brown, silver
- Adhesives: $\frac{1}{8}$" double-sided tape, dimensional adhesive, glue stick
- Buttons (2)
- Craft scissors
- Decorative paper
- Flat-backed marbles: clear, large (12)
- Inkpad: black
- Magnets: $\frac{3}{4}$" circle (12)
- Metal box with lid
- Micro beads: silver
- Mulberry paper: assorted colors to coordinate with decorative paper (5–6)
- Paintbrush: small
- Pencil
- Ribbon: $\frac{1}{2}$" silk
- Rubber stamps: alphabet, desired image
- Ruler
- Tissue paper
- Wire cutters

Instructions

To embellish box

1. Lay box lid, face down, on backside of decorative paper; trace twice, cutting out two pieces.

2. Adhere one piece to front of box lid using glue stick, and one piece to inside of lid.

3. Cut strips of double-sided tape to fit around edges of box lid. Adhere to lid; trim with craft scissors as needed. Expose adhesive of top-facing tape and cover with micro beads. Gently press into tape to secure in place.

4. Stamp desired name or word on center of 6" piece of ribbon; let dry. Adhere ribbon to top of box lid with glue stick.

5. Snip off button shanks using wire cutters. Adhere buttons to ribbon with dimensional adhesive. Set box aside.

Micro beads frame the rim of the flat-backed marbles used to create the magnets. **Opposite:** Magnets are quickly and easily attached with dimensional adhesive.

time-saving tip

Hold Steady

Working on a vellux mat or even a small towel will help immensely as you decorate the magnets. The marbles have a tendency to roll around on a slick surface, which can be quite distracting.

To make marble magnets

1. Cut decorative paper in several pieces, a bit larger than marbles; set aside.

2. Using brown paint, stamp desired image onto tissue paper; let dry.

3. Trim tissue paper images to fit on flat side of marble. Adhere image, face down, to flat side of each marble using small paintbrush and dimensional adhesive.

4. Tear small pieces of mulberry paper. Layer torn pieces behind image and adhere with dimensional adhesive.

5. Using small paintbrush and dimensional adhesive, adhere one piece of decorative paper to back of each marble, making sure decorative side shows through to front of marble. Paint back of each marble with dimensional adhesive; let dry about 20 minutes. For a finished look, paint the back side of each marble with silver acrylic paint; let dry.

6. Trim decorative paper to size of marble using craft scissors.

7. Wrap double-sided tape around each marble. Expose top layer of tape and cover tape with micro beads.

8. Adhere magnet to center of back of each marble using dimensional adhesive; let dry.

9. Place finished marble magnets in decorated box.

time-saving tip

Send a Message

Rather than using a decorative stamp, consider adding a letter to the back of each marble to spell out desired words or message.

Photo Frame

Materials

- 12"x 12" wooden frame
- Charm
- Embossing powder: gold
- Heat tool
- Heavyweight cardstock: patterned
- Pencil
- Photo mat

- Pigment ink: gold
- Ribbon: 1/2" sheer gold
- Rubber stamp: swirl
- Ruler
- Spray adhesive
- Spray paint: coordinating

Instructions

1. Remove glass from frame and spray paint entire frame and frame support; let dry.

2. Place frame face down on patterned cardstock, with backside of cardstock facing up and edges aligned. Using a pencil, trace outline of window for glass.

3. Using gold ink, stamp swirls on front of cardstock. Cover with gold embossing powder and melt powder using heat tool. Allow to cool.

4. Coat back of cardstock with spray adhesive and attach to frame front. *Note:* Do not spray the frame with adhesive.

5. Tie ribbon around left side of frame into a knot. Add an additional 4" piece of ribbon to knot; trim ends and attach charm. Add photo mat and photo, as desired.

time-saving tip

Make It Stick

If your cardstock is lifting from the frame, add another layer of spray adhesive and stack a couple of heavy books on top of the Photo Frame. Let it sit for about 20 minutes to ensure a secure bond.

Clipboard

Materials

- 12" x 14" clipboard: white
- Adhesives: craft glue, double-sided tape, spray adhesive
- Cardstock: double-sided patterned (3); solid color; white
- Craft scissors
- Notepads: medium, small (1 each)
- Paper punch: corner rounder
- Pencil
- Postage stamp booklet
- Ribbon: $\frac{1}{4}$" grosgrain; $\frac{1}{2}$" dotted organdy; 1" coordinating sheer (2)
- Ruler
- Star embellishments: large (1), small (3)

Instructions

1. Measure patterned cardstock and trim so there's an equal border on lower edge and sides of clipboard. Round corners with paper punch on two lower points and attach to board with spray adhesive, centering side to side and aligning along lower edge.

2. Cut matching strip for top of board, rounding upper corners with paper punch. Glue under clip, trimming if necessary. Place grosgrain ribbon over seam and attach with craft glue. Add a touch of glue to ribbon ends to prevent fraying.

3. Cut three rectangles—$4\frac{1}{2}$" x 6" and two 4" x 3" (approximate sizes) out of patterned cardstock. Layer largest rectangle onto white cardstock and trim, leaving $\frac{1}{8}$" border.

4. **To create large pocket:** Attach largest rectangle to left side of board with double-sided tape, applying tape only on each side and lower edge to make pocket.

5. **To decorate larger notepad:** Cut piece of patterned cardstock width of notepad and approximately 3" tall. Fold over top of notepad and secure at back with double-sided tape. Tie dotted organdy ribbon across front flap and glue in place. Adhere small star embellishment to solid color cardstock; trim, leaving $\frac{1}{8}$" border. Adhere on top of ribbon. Slip cardboard backing of notepad into largest pocket.

A nice and neat pocket holds a book of stamps but could also store return address labels.

6. **To create upper right pocket:**
   Tie dotted organdy ribbon around one of the remaining rectangles. Attach to right side of clipboard, applying tape only on each side and lower edge to make pocket. Adhere small star embellishment onto solid color cardstock; trim, leaving ⅛" border. Attach star to pocket. Slip pages of remaining pad into pocket.

7. **To create lower right pocket:**
   Tie dotted organdy ribbon around remaining rectangle. Attach to lower right side of clipboard. Make 2½" square pocket by folding 2½" x 5" piece of patterned cardstock in half. Glue at each side to make pocket and attach to left side of lower right pocket. Glue on small star adhered to solid color cardstock and slip postage stamp book into outer pocket.

8. Adhere large embellishment onto solid color cardstock; trim to ⅛" border. Attach with double-sided tape to center of clip. Tie 6" lengths of coordinating sheer ribbons around clip.

While we decorated the metal portion of the clipboard with a star embellishment, you could easily tie on 6" lengths of various ribbons.

time-saving tip

Fool the Eye

To conserve ribbon on pockets, cut ribbon approximately 1" longer than cardstock to be wrapped. Tape ends to backside of cardstock to form a band on the front, then tie an additional piece of ribbon around the band in either a knot or bow. The knot or bow can be moved across the band for perfect alignment when your project is complete.

Birdhouse

Materials

- ¾" circle punch
- Acrylic paint: assorted colors, teal
- Cardstock: copper
- Craft glue
- Craft scissors
- Paintbrushes: assorted sizes
- Paper towel or soft cloth
- Papier-mâché birdhouse
- Spray paint: white

Instructions

1. Spray birdhouse white; let dry completely.

2. Paint house desired color, leaving windows, doors, and trim white.

3. Paint flowers around base of house.

4. Thin teal paint slightly with water and, working quickly, paint a wash over entire house, one panel at a time, wiping off paint with paper towel or soft cloth.

5. Punch ¾" circles from copper cardstock. Align on roof, beginning at lower edge and overlapping slightly, and adhere with craft glue. Using craft scissors, trim circles as necessary to fit around chimney.

6. Cut strips of copper cardstock to fit roof point and chimney top.

Matchboxes

Materials

- Craft scissors
- Decorative paper: coordinating prints (3)
- Decorative trim: pom-pom
- Glue stick
- Matchboxes (3)
- Pencil
- Ruler

Instructions

1. Remove tray inside each matchbox so you are left with the outer box. Measure outside surface and cut out that shape from decorative paper.

2. Wrap decorative paper around each box; secure in place with glue stick.

3. Measure sides of each matchbox tray that will be visible. Trace those two shapes on decorative paper; cut out.

4. Adhere paper to sides of each tray using glue stick. Cut out elements from decorative paper and glue on coordinating prints. Adhere decorative trim.

time-saving tip

Use the Leftovers

Get creative! Add frills (such as pom-pom trim) or pretty ribbon to the boxes. If you are decorating several sets of matchboxes, mix and match your decorative papers, cutting out elements to embellish as we've done here.

Pillar Candle

Materials

- 8" glass pillar candle
- Adhesives: acid-free adhesive dispenser, foam dots
- Cardstock: brown, green
- Computer, printer, and scanner
- Decorative paper: coordinating pattern, pink-and-brown striped
- Paper trimmer
- Photograph
- Ribbon: $\frac{1}{4}$" green satin, $\frac{1}{4}$" pink rickrack
- Ruler
- Scissors: craft, decorative-edge

Instructions

1. Cut 9" x 4" piece of green cardstock. Wrap around pillar candle, overlapping in back and securing with adhesive dispenser.

2. Cut 9" x 2$\frac{3}{4}$" piece of pink-and-brown striped paper. Layer on top of green cardstock, overlapping in back and securing in place with adhesive dispenser.

3. Cut 9" length of green ribbon. Wrap around candle, overlapping in back.

4. Cut 2" x $\frac{1}{2}$" piece of brown cardstock using decorative-edge scissors. Cut strip of pattern decorative paper to 2$\frac{1}{2}$" using decorative-edge scissors. Layer on brown cardstock, folding edges to back, and adhere on ribbon using foam dots.

5. Scan desired photograph in computer and print at 1$\frac{1}{4}$" x 1". Trim printed photograph and adhere on top of brown cardstock using foam dots.

6. Cut two 9" pieces of pink rickrack. Adhere along top and bottom of green cardstock, securing in place with adhesive dispenser.

7. Cut 11" piece of green ribbon. Wrap around top of pillar candle and tie into knot; trim ends.

Placemats

Materials

- Bamboo placemats (4)
- Permanent ink: green
- Ribbon: 1/2" satin
- Rubber stamp: large swirl

Instructions

1. Stamp swirl design in opposite corners of placemats; let dry completely.

2. Stamp 1 yard length of ribbon with same stamp; let dry completely.

3. Roll placemats so that one stamped corner shows and tie with ribbon.

time-saving tip

Steady as You Go

To ensure a clean stamped image, use a large ceramic tile, at least an 8" square, as a sturdy base under your stamping surface.

CHAPTER 5

The dizzying scope of bead types available is gift inspiration just waiting to be tapped. Girls of any age will appreciate a gift with a little "bling." Beaded earrings are sure to delight a sister, niece, or girlfriend. Craft a lovely necklace for a graduate or bride-to-be. If you are the bride, create matching necklaces for each bridesmaid. Commemorate a milestone with a unique bracelet, personalizing it with a charm specific to the event. Fashion a matching set of earrings, necklace, and bracelet to really wow the recipient. Not all beaded gifts must be jewelry, however. An avid reader will appreciate a beautifully beaded bookmark slipped between the pages of a gripping new novel. There are gorgeous gifts aplenty throughout this chapter.

Pink & Brown Necklace

Materials

- Beading wire: 0.16 diameter silver
- Crimp beads: sterling silver (2)
- Drop bead: large pink quartz
- Facetted round crystal beads: pink (12)
- Shell beads: bronze rectangle (24)
- Strand of tourmaline chips
- Toggle clasp: sterling silver

Tools

- Bent-nose pliers
- Wire cutters

Instructions

1. Cinch crimp bead on end of 2-foot length of beading wire, leaving about 2½" of excess wire.

2. Begin stringing beads in this sequence: 12 tourmaline chips, 1 bronze shell bead, 1 facetted crystal bead, and 1 shell bronze bead. Continue this pattern six times.

3. Add 4 tourmaline chips followed by large pink quartz bead.

4. Mirror same pattern on other side and crimp to secure tightly. Loosen crimp bead and make any adjustments if necessary.

5. Feed beading wire through toggle clasp and cinch crimp bead. Pull tight and crimp tightly with bent-nose pliers.

6. Repeat step 5 on other side of necklace with remaining side of toggle clasp. Cut excess wire on both sides.

Pearl Drop Lariat

Materials

- Beading wire: 0.16 diameter silver
- Chain: 1" sterling silver
- Crimp beads: sterling silver (2)
- Drop pins with decorative bottom: small (5)
- Facetted round beads: bronze (13)
- Potato pearls: medium brown (8); medium peach (23); small white (30)
- Round bead: sterling silver
- Strand of garnet chips

Tools

- Bent-nose pliers
- Round-nose pliers
- Wire cutters

Instructions

1. **To make pearl drop:** Slide 4 peach potato pearls onto drop pins (1 per pin) and 1 pin with 3 garnet chips.

2. Using round-nose pliers, make small loop in drop pin at top of beads.

3. Slide end of drop pin through chain links (1 per link).

4. Wrap excess wire around base of loops to secure in place; cut excess wire.

5. Feed 2-foot piece of beading wire through top link in chain and crimp tightly using crimping bead.

6. Begin beading necklace in this sequence: 3 garnet chips, 2 white potato pearls, 2 bronze facetted beads, 2 peach potato pearls, 15 garnet chips, 2 brown potato pearls, 1 bronze facetted bead, 2 white potato pearls, 2 peach potato pearls, 10 garnet chips, 1 potato pearl, 1 brown potato pearl, 2 peach potato pearls, 1 bronze facetted bead, 2 white potato pearls, 1 bronze facetted bead, 12 garnet chips, 2 peach potato pearls, 2 bronze facetted beads, 1 peach potato pearl, 2 brown potato pearls, 3 white potato pearls, 11 garnet chips, 1 brown potato pearl, 1 peach potato pearl, 1 bronze facetted bead, 2 peach potato pearls, 9 garnet chips, 2 peach potato pearls, 1 brown potato pearl, 2 white potato pearls, 2 bronze facetted beads, 7 garnet chips, 2 peach potato pearls, 1 brown potato pearl, 5 garnet chips, 1 bronze facetted bead, 1 peach potato pearl,

Left: The drop can also serve as the back of the necklace, allowing the wearer to lengthen the necklace just a bit. **Right:** The hoop at the end of the Pearl Drop Lariat is made with 15 small white potato pearls.

2 white potato pearls, 4 garnet chips, 2 peach potato pearls, 2 bronze facetted beads, 2 white potato pearls, 3 garnet chips, and 1 sterling silver round bead.

7. Cinch crimp after sterling silver bead.

8. String on 15 white potato pearls and make a small loop. Make sure it is big enough for pearl drops to fit.

9. Loosen crimp and slide end of beading wire where your loop is back through and crimp tightly; cut excess wire.

time-saving tip

Avoid Mistakes

Good lighting and magnification will help you bead the perfect project, and limit frustration. If necessary, use a personal task light with magnifier to make beading easier.

Hoop Dangle Earrings

Materials

- Beads: sterling silver (2)
- Drop pins with decorative bottom: small (2)
- Hoop earrings: sterling silver (2)
- Spacers: sterling silver (4)

Tools

- Round-nose pliers
- Wire cutters

Instructions

1. Thread sterling silver spacer onto drop pin and then sterling silver bead. Add second sterling silver spacer on top.

2. Using round-nose pliers, make loop at top of beads and wrap excess wire around base to secure.

3. Cut excess wire and slide onto earring hoop.

4. Repeat steps for second earring.

time-saving tip

Switch It Out

You can wire wrap several different kinds of stones on various drop pins. After you have one pair of hoop earrings you can change out the stones to match different outfits.

Beaded Bookmark

Materials

- Beading wire: .30 diameter silver
- Crimp beads: sterling silver (3)
- Crystal beads: oval (8)
- Facetted drop stone: large teardrop
- Facetted round beads: bronze (6)
- Jump ring: sterling silver
- Ribbon: 1/2" brown silk
- Shell rectangle beads (4)

Tools

- Bent-nose pliers
- Wire cutters

Instructions

1. Slide large drop stone onto 1' length of beading wire until you reach the middle of the wire.

2. Slide 2 oval crystal beads on each side of drop.

3. Slide both sides of beading wire through crimp bead. Pull tight and crimp to secure.

4. Slide both sides of beading wire through bronze facetted bead.

5. Add 1 shell bead, 1 bronze facetted bead, 1 shell bead, and 1 crystal bead on each side of beading wire.

6. Slide both sides of beading wire through 1 bronze facetted bead.

7. Slide both sides of beading wire through crimp bead. Pull tight and crimp to secure.

8. Finish beading with 1 crystal oval bead, 1 bronze facetted bead, 1 crystal oval bead, and 1 bronze facetted bead.

9. Slide on crimp bead and make small loop with beading wire. Feed back through crimp bead and crimp tightly; cut excess wire.

10. Using bent-nose pliers, open jump ring. Slide loop of beading wire onto jump ring. Bend back into place with pliers.

11. Feed 1 foot of ribbon through jump ring. Pull it through until half way mark and tie into a knot.

Drop Earrings

Materials

- Beading wire: .42 diameter soft sterling silver

- Drop pins with loop on end: sterling silver (2)

- Earring loops: sterling silver (2)

- Facetted round beads: bronze (2)

- Teardrop beads: turquoise (2)

- Tube beads: 1" pink quartz (2)

Tools

- Round-nose pliers

- Wire cutters

Instructions

1. Thread bronze bead on drop pin. Add quartz tube bead on top.

2. Using round-nose pliers, make small loop at top of quartz bead and clip excess wire.

3. Feed 1" piece of wire through top of turquoise bead. Pinch wire together at top and make small loop.

4. Slide loop through loop on end of drop pin and wrap excess wire around bottom to secure tightly; clip excess wire with wire cutters.

5. Using pliers, open loop on earring pin. Put circle at top of earring through loop and close tightly with pliers.

6. Repeat steps for second earring.

time-saving tip

Mastering Jewelry Making

Never has jewelry making been so accessible. Craft wire and jewelry wire, pliers, beads, stones, and clasps are all readily available at craft stores, and many of these stores even teach classes for those who want to learn the basics.

Medallion Bracelet

Materials

- Beading wire: 0.16 diameter silver
- Center stone: large rectangle
- Crimp beads: sterling silver (4)
- Facetted round beads: bronze (6)
- Garnet chips (6)
- Strand of quartz chips: small yellow
- Toggle clasp: sterling silver

Tools

- Bent-nose pliers
- Wire cutters

Instructions

1. Put both strands of beading wire together and slide on crimp bead. Crimp tightly, leaving 2" of excess at end for clasp.

2. Slide 1 bronze facetted bead onto both strands of wire. Separate wire and add 8 yellow quartz chips on each side. Finish sequence with 1 bronze facetted bead and 3 garnet chips over both strands. Separate wire and add 8 yellow quartz chips on each side.

3. Add large center stone and mirror other side with same pattern.

4. Check length by putting around wrist to measure.

5. Cut one wire at crimp bead and slide crimp bead on remaining wire.

6. Add one side of toggle clasp and loop beading wire back through crimp bead. Crimp tight to hold.

7. Repeat step 6 on other side with remaining side of toggle clasp; cut excess wire.

Triple-Strand Bracelet

Materials

- Beading wire: 0.16 diameter
- Crimp beads: sterling silver (6)
- Facetted crystal beads: teardrop (12)
- Potato pearls: medium brown (13); medium pink (16); small white (32)
- Round beads: sterling silver (8)
- Toggle clasp with three loops attached: sterling silver

Tools

- Bent-nose pliers
- Wire cutters

Instructions

1. Slide crimp bead on 1-foot length of beading wire. Feed it through one of holes on toggle clasp. Feed back through crimp bead and crimp tightly.

2. String beads in this sequence: 1 sterling silver round bead, 3 white potato pearls, 2 pink potato pearls, 1 brown potato pearl, 1 crystal teardrop bead (large side on first), 1 sterling silver round bead, 1 crystal teardrop bead (small side first), 1 brown potato pearl, 1 pink potato pearl, 1 brown potato pearl, 1 pink potato pearl, 3 white potato pearls, 1 crystal teardrop bead, 1 sterling silver round bead, 1 crystal teardrop bead, 1 pink potato pearl, 2 brown potato pearls, 3 white potato pearls, 1 sterling silver round bead.

3. Slide another crimp bead on and feed through same loop on other side of toggle clasp. Crimp tightly to secure. Check length.

4. Put second piece of 1-foot length of beading wire through second loop and crimp tightly to secure.

5. String beads in this sequence: 3 white potato pearls, 1 sterling silver round bead, 2 brown potato pearls, 3 white potato pearls, 1 crystal teardrop bead, 1 pink potato pearl, 1 crystal teardrop bead, 2 white potato pearls, 1 crystal teardrop bead, 1 pink potato pearl, 1 crystal teardrop bead, 3 white potato pearls, 1 brown potato pearl, 2 pink potato pearls, 1 sterling silver round bead, 3 white potato pearls.

6. Repeat step 3.

Whether you're designing a bracelet or a necklace, there are four basic designs to keep in mind.

A Random—Mixture of beads, patterns, and even color.

B Repeating—Forms a pattern of shapes (and color) and repeats it every inch or so.

C Asymmetrical—Almost a lopsided approach. The two sides are set in an uneven pattern.

D Symmetrical—Well-porportioned and regular in form.

7. Put third 1-foot length of beading wire through last loop on toggle clasp and crimp tightly.

8. String beads in this sequence: 1 sterling silver round bead, 3 white potato pearls, 1 brown potato pearl, 2 pink potato pearls, 1 crystal teardrop bead, 1 brown potato pearl, 1 crystal teardrop bead, 1 pink potato pearl, 2 brown potato pearls, 1 pink potato pearl, 3 white potato pearls, 1 crystal teardrop bead, 1 pink potato pearl, 1 crystal teardrop bead, 2 pink potato pearls, 1 brown potato pearl, 3 white potato pearls, 1 sterling silver round bead.

9. Repeat step 3. Cut excess wire.

A silver toggle clasp not only serves a functional purpose; it also complements the silver accents of the bracelet.

time-saving tip
Crimp to Secure

When beading multi-strand bracelets or necklaces, if you cut the wire long enough you can secure the first strand with a crimp bead at the very end. This will keep the beads from sliding off while you bead the other strands.

3-Strand Necklace

Materials

- Beading wire: 0.16 diameter
- Crimp beads: sterling silver (12)
- Jump rings: sterling silver (2)
- Lobster clasp: sterling silver
- Split ring: sterling silver
- Strand of black onyx ovals
- Strand of 1" pink quartz wafer stones
- Strand of small tourmaline rectangles

Tools

- Bent-nose pliers
- Needle-nose pliers
- Wire cutters

Instructions

1. Slide 2-foot length of beading wire through crimp bead. Crimp tightly, leaving 2" of excess wire for clasp.

2. String on 18 pink wafer stones. Crimp end tightly.

3. Repeat step 1. String on tourmaline rectangles to desired length and crimp end tightly.

4. Repeat step 1. String on black onyx ovals to desired length and crimp tightly at end.

5. Loop excess wire on all three strands one at a time through jump ring and crimp tightly to secure. Repeat this step with opposite end of beading wire with remaining jump ring.

6. Using bent-nose and needle-nose pliers, open split ring and slide on lobster clasp and one jump ring. Close split ring tightly. Check length and cut excess wire.

time-saving tip

Two are Better Than One

To open a jump ring easily, use two pairs of pliers, such as a flat-nose and chain-nose, and grasp the jump ring on either side of the opening. Gently pull one of the pliers and side of the ring toward you and the other away from you until it's open far enough to use in the project. To close, do the opposite, pulling inward until the ends of the ring meet.

CHAPTER 6

Half the fun of giving a gift is creating the wrapping. Gift wrap can be personalized for the recipient or the occasion. It can even hint at the gift inside. You can create a stack of gift boxes using a simple pattern and coordinating decorative papers and then fill each one with a surprise. Or maybe fashion a unique bag featuring vintage images and gorgeous ribbon. An embellished tea canister filled with a selection of tea and embellished with a demitasse spoon for stirring is a thoughtful get-well gift. You can even create a presentation for a gift card using a simple handmade envelope or a file folder that's also a tribute to the recipient. The ideas are endless but in this chapter there is something that's guaranteed to get your creative juices flowing.

Stacked Gift Boxes

Materials

- Adhesives: acid-free adhesive dispenser, craft glue, hook-and-loop self-adhesive dots
- Buttons (6)
- Craft scissors
- Embroidery floss
- Heavyweight cardstock: coordinating double-sided patterned (6)
- Pencil
- Ribbon: $5/8$" organdy
- Ruler
- Scoring tool

Instructions

Note: All boxes are 1" deep. Diameters of boxes increase in $1/2$" increments. On the template, only box A and box B change in diameter; all flaps remain 1" wide, but expand in length according to the size of A and B.

1. With six different double-sided pieces of cardstock, cut the following rectangles: 3" x 5" for 1" box; 4" x 7" for 2" box; $4^1/2$" x 8" for $2^1/2$" box; 5" x 9" for 3" box; $5^1/2$" x 10" for $3^1/2$" box; and 6" x 11" for 4" box.

2. With scoring tool, score each rectangle 1" from all edges. Score each across the width at the size of A/B (see Stacked Boxes template, page 104) plus 1" (for example, if making the 4" box, score at 5" from each end). Cut on all solid lines and score at all dashed lines. Trim flap according to diagram.

3. Fold into lidded box shape and then adhere corners with adhesive dispenser. *Note:* Trim flap corners if necessary to fold box neatly. The angled flap will remain outside of the box front.

time-saving tip

Unbutton the Box

To save a few minutes, tuck the box's front flap inside the box. This will eliminate the need to apply a decorative button and hook-and-loop dot.

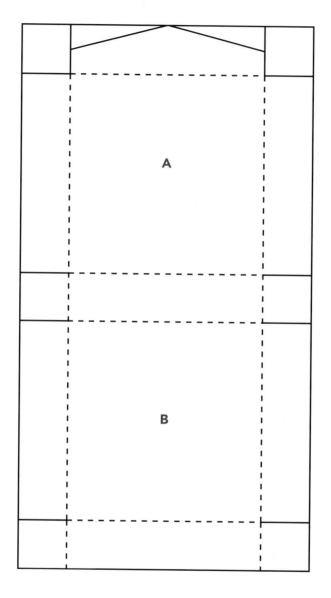

Stacked Boxes Template
Enlarge 175%

4. Apply self-adhesive hook-and-fastener dot to underside of angled flap. Tie 24" length of embroidery floss through holes in button; knot and trim excess. Adhere to front of flap with craft glue.

5. Stack boxes and wrap with 2 yards of ribbon, tying bow on top.

Buttons are quickly added to the Stacked Gift Boxes with craft glue. The front flaps are held closed with hook-and-loop self-adhesive dots.

time-saving tip

Go Heavy to Hold

If the contents of the Stacked Gift Boxes are somewhat heavy, use thicker-weight, double-sided cardstock to create sturdier boxes.

Beribboned Gift Bag

Materials

- ½" hole punch
- 4" x 6" vintage postcard
- Adhesives: ½" double-sided tape, glue stick
- Cosmetic sponge
- Eyelet setting tools
- Eyelets: silver
- Glitter: ultra-fine blue
- Heavyweight cardstock: white
- Inkpad: light brown
- Pencil
- Ribbon: 1" satin
- Ruler
- Scissors: craft, decorative-edge
- Scoring tool

Instructions

1. Copy Gift Bag template (page 108) onto cardstock. Cut, score, and fold into gift bag shape. Trim top edge with decorative-edge scissors.

2. Referring to template, mark placement for holes along sides of gift bag. Using the setting tools, set eyelets in these holes.

3. Refold gift bag, then punch 10 evenly spaced holes along bottom of bag, ½" up from bottom. Set eyelets in these holes.

time-saving tip

Picture Perfect

To personalize the gift bag, use a picture of the recipient in place of the postcard.

Beribboned Gift Bag Template

Enlarge 225%

4. Trim edges of postcard with double-sided tape and sprinkle on glitter. Adhere postcard to front of gift bag using glue stick.

5. Working from back to front, thread 12" length of ribbon through eyelets at bottom of gift bag; tie ends in a bow.

6. Working from bottom to top, thread 30" length of ribbon through eyelets at back of gift bag; tie ends in a bow.

7. Using hole punch, punch hole 1" down each side of gift bag. Tie 15" length of ribbon in holes.

8. Using inkpad and cosmetic sponge, color edges of gift bag.

A lace-up effect makes the back of the Beribboned Gift Bag just as pretty as the front.

time-saving tip

Alter the Backside

Rather than add eyelets and lace up the back of the Beribboned Gift Bag, adhere the back with a glue stick and layer the seam with a length of ribbon. This will save time without reducing the charm.

Gift Box

Materials

- Cardstock: 12" x 12" double-sided patterned (2 sheets); brown
- Craft glue
- Craft scissors
- Feather: white
- Inkpad: brown
- Paper punch: corner rounder
- Pencil
- Ribbon: ½" brown grosgrain
- Rubber stamps: bird (2–3)
- Ruler
- Scoring tool

Instructions

1. Cut patterned cardstock into following pieces: four 2¾" squares, four 2¼" squares, two 12" x 2¾" strips, and 6" x 12" piece scored at 3" and 6".

2. Measure and score 3" from each edge of second piece of 12" x 12" cardstock. Cut along score lines 3" from left and right sides.

3. Fold along remaining score lines. Trace Gift Box template (page 112) onto brown cardstock to create box base; cut out and score on fold lines. Glue in place.

time-saving tip

Finish with Fun Touches

To coordinate the inside with the outside, stamp the tissue paper to be placed inside the gift box. Top it with an embossed image raised with large glue dots for a three-dimensional effect.

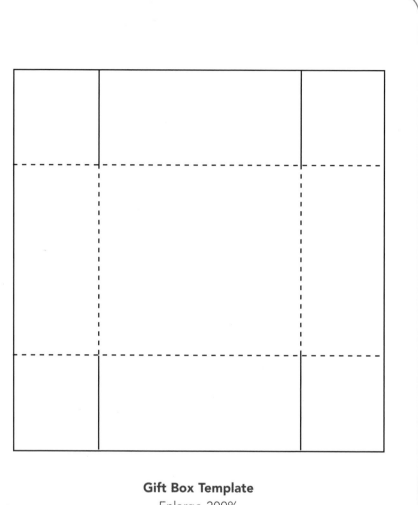

Gift Box Template
Enlarge 200%

A white feather makes a great finishing touch but could easily be omitted from the project.

4. Wrap and glue 12" x 2¾" strips around side of box, overlapping and securing ends near center of box sides.

5. Stamp bird images on small squares and layer on remaining squares. Glue one square to box front on lower half of square to form a holder for box lid. Glue remaining squares to sides and back of box.

6. Glue lid to inside of box back, lining up 3" score line with top of box. Fold along remaining score line. Round corners with paper punch.

7. Tie 1 yard of ribbon around center of box lid and attach feather. Slip lid front into square to close.

time-saving tip

From Plain to Pretty Cool

If you have a sheet of generic print or solid cardstock that you want to use, but want to customize it for a special occasion, stamp images relevant to the event in dye ink all over the paper before cutting and folding. Use these same images for the embellishments on the box sides and top to really make this project come together.

Gift Card Holder

Materials

- A4 envelope
- Adhesives: double-sided tape, glue dots
- Cardstock: decorative print
- Cosmetic sponge
- Craft scissors
- Decorative paper scrap
- Foil tape: silver
- Glass slide: 1½" square
- Inkpad: coordinating
- Ribbon: silver metallic

Instructions

1. Fold envelope in half. Open and cut flap from point to envelope top.

2. With backside of envelope facing up, seal left flap.

3. Ink edges of envelope using cosmetic sponge. Trim cardstock to wrap around front and back of envelope and adhere in place with double-sided tape.

4. Cut cardstock to fit inside left side of envelope and adhere with double-sided tape.

5. Cut two pieces of rectangular cardstock to fit right flap and adhere front and back of right flap.

6. Adhere cardstock to lower half of inside right of envelope.

7. Wrap 18" length of ribbon around cardstock and tie on right front of gift card holder, if desired; trim ends.

8. Trim scrap of decorative paper to fit glass slide. Wrap edges in silver tape to secure. Attach glass slide over ribbon on card front with glue dots.

Invite Out

Materials

- Acid-free adhesive dispenser
- Cardstock: cream, white
- Decorative paper: coordinating prints (3)
- Jewel: adhesive-backed heart
- Paper trimmer
- Ribbon: $1/8$" multi-colored, $1/4$" orange grosgrain
- Ruler
- Scissors: craft, decorative-edge
- Sticker: initial letter
- Tickets to favorite play, musical, sporting event, etc.

Instructions

1. Cut 4" x $8^1/2$" piece of white cardstock. Cut $3^1/2$" x 8" piece of decorative paper; adhere to white cardstock with adhesive dispenser.

2. Cut 6" x $3^1/2$" piece of coordinating decorative paper. Cut 6" x $1^1/2$" piece of another coordinating decorative paper; adhere to decorative paper. Wrap decorative paper band around bottom of cardstock base, securing at very bottom and at back with adhesive dispenser.

3. Cut 10" length of grosgrain ribbon. Wrap around layered decorative paper band, tying in a knot at front.

4. Cut 3" x 7" piece of coordinating paper. Adhere initial sticker at top and then tie with multi-colored ribbon and embellish with heart rhinestone. Insert tickets in invite pocket.

time-saving tip

Hold It in Place

To prevent the ribbon from sliding off the bottom of the invitation base, add a dab of glue on the backside to hold it in place.

Bottle Carrier

Materials

- Adhesives: acid-free adhesive dispenser, masking tape
- Craft scissors
- Decorative papers
- Drink bottles with carrier
- Pencil
- Ribbon: ½" coordinating (2)
- Rub-on images and applicator
- Ruler
- Spray paint: white

Instructions

1. If labeling filled bottles, mask all but caps with masking tape. If labeling empty bottles, remove caps. Spray paint caps and carrier white; repeat coat if needed.

2. Using side of carrier as a template, trace and cut decorative papers to fit; adhere to carrier with adhesive dispenser. Cut 1" strip of decorative paper and adhere around circumference of carrier. Tie several 6" lengths of ribbon through carrier handle; knot to secure and then trim ends.

3. Embellish bottles by adhering strips of paper around glass centers with adhesive dispenser. *Note:* The paper strips can be inscribed with the recipient's name, if desired.

4. Decorate bottle caps with rub-on images and strips of decorative paper; fill with desired beverage. *Note:* You may also want to apply project instructions to cover purchased bottles already filled.

Tea Tin

Materials

- Adhesives: glue stick, spray adhesive
- Cardstock: coordinating self-adhesive strips; patterned cardstock; solid color
- Craft scissors
- Craft wire: silver
- Demitasse spoon
- Paper punch: large circle (to fit tin lid)
- Pen: metallic
- Ribbon: ½" grosgrain
- Ruler
- Spray paint: white
- Stickers: cup, saucer, spoon, teapot
- Tea
- Tea tin
- Wire cutters

Instructions

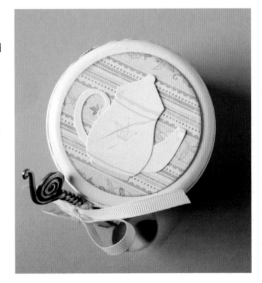

1. Remove tin lid and spray paint lid and base white.

2. Spray patterned cardstock with adhesive and wrap around tin base to cover. Place coordinating cardstock strips as desired on tin base and lid.

3. Cut out two tag shapes from same patterned cardstock and from solid color cardstock, one slightly smaller than the other. Adhere with glue stick.

4. Attach cup, saucer, and spoon stickers to tag. *Note:* The spoon color can be altered with a metallic pen.

5. Punch circle out of patterned cardstock using paper punch; adhere to tin lid using spray adhesive. Attach teapot sticker.

6. Tie ribbon around tin and attach spoon. Attach tag to spoon with 5" length of wire. Add favorite tea.

Gift Card Folder

Materials

- ¼", 1", 1¼" circle punches
- Adhesives: craft glue, double-sided tape
- Cardstock: coordinating double-sided patterned (2); coordinating solid color; white
- Computer and printer (optional)
- Craft scissors
- Decorative paper
- Holiday photos
- Inkpad: coordinating color
- Ribbon: ¼" gold metallic
- Ruler
- Stamp: holiday-related

Instructions

1. Cut solid cardstock into 3" square and 3" x 6" piece for each photo you'll be using. Cut white cardstock to 2½" square. Cut decorative paper to 2¾" square (for cover) and various sizes to fit photos for inside Gift Card Folder.

2. Trace two file folder shapes (see Gift Card Folder template, page 124) on double-sided cardstock; cut out. Layer so that folder tabs are staggered. Punch ¼" holes in spine and tie together with 1 yard of gold ribbon.

3. Stamp image on white cardstock and layer onto decorative paper and cardstock squares.

4. Punch 1" circle from patterned cardstock or paper and layer onto 1¼" solid cardstock. Attach to left side of stamped image and layer all onto front of Gift Card Folder.

5. Using double-sided tape, layer photos onto printed cardstock and add to inside of Gift Card Folder. Add computer or hand-written journaling, if desired.

6. Fold 3" x 6" piece of solid color cardstock in half to 3" x 3"; glue sides together to form pocket. Fold edge to bottom, then attached to inside back cover.

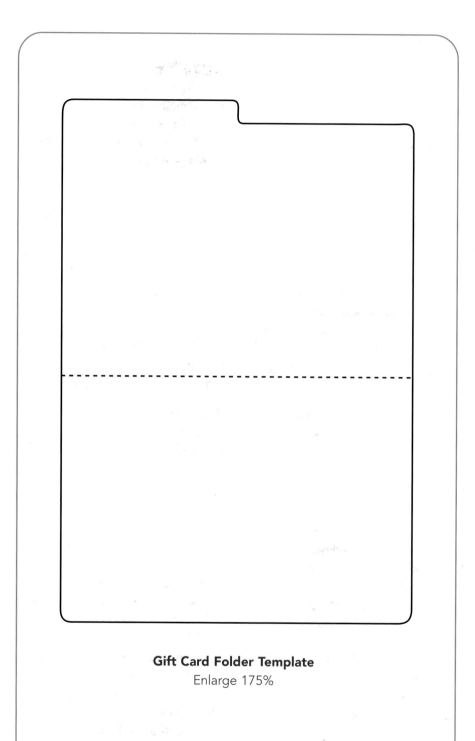

Gift Card Folder Template
Enlarge 175%

Contributors

Destiny Stones

Pages 82 – 99

Cassie Berrett, Brandy Shay, Tiffani Nye, and Rachelle Clausse share many things in addition to a love of jewelry. They are four sisters who together craft beautiful beaded pieces inspired by their mother, who always carried stones in her pockets because she believed in the metaphysical properties each one held. In their mother's memory, they started Destiny Stones, a purveyor of one-of-a-kind jewelry. Each semi-precious stone is hand picked and thoughtfully married to create unique necklaces, bracelets, and earrings. Destiny Stones jewelry is sold in retail stores throughout the United States.

Sunday Hendrickson

Pages 24, 28, 30, 46, 50, 52, 54, 56, 74

Sunday Hendrickson is a well-known photo stylist, field editor, and producer. She has worked for a wide variety of clients including *Country Living*, *Home Magazine*, *Coastal Living*, *Family Circle*, *Woman's Day*, *Good Housekeeping*, and *Mary Engelbreit's Home Companion*, to name just a few. She earned a Bachelor of Arts degree in Journalism from Pennsylvania State University and studied at the School of Visual Arts and Parsons School of Design, both in New York. Sunday has been the design director for *Ladies Home Journal*, art director for *Modern Bride* magazine, and creative director for Lovelace Publications.

Sunday lives in Los Angeles, California.

Rebecca Ittner

Pages 32, 62, 106

Rebecca Ittner is a freelance photo stylist, editor, and writer based in Southern California. She has spent the last decade traveling around the country working with artists and authors, helping to bring their dreams to print.

A lifelong love of collecting and crafting continues to bring her joy. Fueled by the genius and inspiration of the women she works with, Rebecca spends any spare time creating—from altered art and books to decoupage and woodworking. Her creations reflect her passions, including family, love, nature, the arts, and travel.

Rebecca lives in Tustin, California.

Roxi Phillips

Pages 22, 26, 36, 38, 42, 44, 102, 118

Roxi Phillips is an award-winning paper and mixed-media artist who has dabbled in a wide variety of crafts throughout her life. Her eclectic style and diversity is shown in her work, from altered art projects to more traditional scrapbooking.

Roxi designs paper art projects for several companies including Krylon and Tapestry by CR Gibson. Her work is featured regularly in national magazines such as *Scrapbooking and Beyond*, *PaperCrafts*, and *PaperWorks*, and crafting books including *Spray Paint Paper Crafts: Creative Fun with Krylon* (©2007, Sterling Publishing, Inc.).

Roxi and her family live in western Tennessee.

Catherine Risling

Pages 60, 76, 116

Catherine Risling is a talented and experienced journalist who has worked with some of the most dynamic designers in the craft and home décor industries. Rubbing elbows with these talents has nurtured her creative spirit and led her to consult on countless projects, designs, and photo shoots.

Her first book, *Pretty Weddings for Practically Pennies* (©2005, Sterling Publishing, Inc.), included many original and budget-conscious projects she created for her own wedding. She is also the author of *Make It in Minutes: Wedding Crafts* (©2008, Sterling Publishing, Inc.).

Cathy is the director of editorial for Red Lips 4 Courage Communications, Inc., a book producer for Lark Books and Sterling Publishing, Inc. She has worked on several major metropolitan newspapers and was the executive managing editor of *Romantic Homes* and *Victorian Homes* magazines for several years.

Cathy lives in Southern California with her husband, Greg.

Candice Windham

Pages 48, 66, 68, 72, 78, 110, 114, 120, 122

Graphic designer, altered artist, paper crafter, rubber stamp artist, painter, and teacher, Candice Windham's work has appeared in various books and publications, including magazines *Altered Arts* and the premier issue of *Make It Mine*. She is also a museum curator and designer, which allows her to combine her love of history and art. She is represented by the Rivertown Gallery in downtown Memphis, Tennessee.

Candice lives in Brighton, Tennessee, with her husband, Larry, son Michael, and pups, Pete and Sam.

METRIC EQUIVALENCY CHARTS

inches to millimeters and centimeters
(mm-millimeters, cm-centimeters)

inches	mm	cm	inches	cm	inches	cm
1/8	3	0.3	9	22.9	30	76.2
1/4	6	0.6	10	25.4	31	78.7
1/2	13	1.3	12	30.5	33	83.8
5/8	16	1.6	13	33.0	34	86.4
3/4	19	1.9	14	35.6	35	88.9
7/8	22	2.2	15	38.1	36	91.4
1	25	2.5	16	40.6	37	94.0
1 1/4	32	3.2	17	43.2	38	96.5
1 1/2	38	3.8	18	45.7	39	99.1
1 3/4	44	4.4	19	48.3	40	101.6
2	51	5.1	20	50.8	41	104.1
2 1/2	64	6.4	21	53.3	42	106.7
3	76	7.6	22	55.9	43	109.2
3 1/2	89	8.9	23	58.4	44	111.8
4	102	10.2	24	61.0	45	114.3
4 1/2	114	11.4	25	63.5	46	116.8
5	127	12.7	26	66.0	47	119.4
6	152	15.2	27	68.6	48	121.9
7	178	17.8	28	71.1	49	124.5
8	203	20.3	29	73.7	50	127.0

yards to meters

yards	meters	yards	meters	yards	meters	yards	meters	yards	meters
1/8	0.11	2 1/8	1.94	4 1/8	3.77	6 1/8	5.60	8 1/8	7.43
1/4	0.23	2 1/4	2.06	4 1/4	3.89	6 1/4	5.72	8 1/4	7.54
3/8	0.34	2 3/8	2.17	4 3/8	4.00	6 3/8	5.83	8 3/8	7.66
1/2	0.46	2 1/2	2.29	4 1/2	4.11	6 1/2	5.94	8 1/2	7.77
5/8	0.57	2 5/8	2.40	4 5/8	4.23	6 5/8	6.06	8 5/8	7.89
3/4	0.69	2 3/4	2.51	4 3/4	4.34	6 3/4	6.17	8 3/4	8.00
7/8	0.80	2 7/8	2.63	4 7/8	4.46	6 7/8	6.29	8 7/8	8.12
1	0.91	3	2.74	5	4.57	7	6.40	9	8.23
1 1/8	1.03	3 1/8	2.86	5 1/8	4.69	7 1/8	6.52	9 1/8	8.34
1 1/4	1.14	3 1/4	2.97	5 1/4	4.80	7 1/4	6.63	9 1/4	8.46
1 3/8	1.26	3 3/8	3.09	5 3/8	4.91	7 3/8	6.74	9 3/8	8.57
1 1/2	1.37	3 1/2	3.20	5 1/2	5.03	7 1/2	6.86	9 1/2	8.69
1 5/8	1.49	3 5/8	3.31	5 5/8	5.14	7 5/8	6.97	9 5/8	8.80
1 3/4	1.60	3 3/4	3.43	5 3/4	5.26	7 3/4	7.09	9 3/4	8.92
1 7/8	1.71	3 7/8	3.54	5 7/8	5.37	7 7/8	7.20	9 7/8	9.03
2	1.83	4	3.66	6	5.49	8	7.32	10	9.14

INDEX